This Book Belongs To

Assalamu alaikum dear friends!

Are you ready for an exciting Ramadan adventure?

This Ramadan Activity Book is specially made for you, with over 90 fun and creative activities to help you make the most of this special month.

Ramadan is a time for reflection, self-improvement, and growing closer to Allah (SWT). It is the perfect opportunity to learn new things, try new things, and set some goals for yourself. This book is here to help you do just that!

You'll find all sorts of activities inside, like coloring pages, word searches, mazes, and drawing prompts. You'll also have the chance to set your own Ramadan goals and track your progress as you work towards them.

We know you're going to have a great time with this book, so let's get started! Get your pen and markers ready, and let's see what kind of amazing things you can create.

Remember, the most important thing is to have fun and enjoy this special time with your family and friends.

Ramadan Day 1

My Fasting Today Was:

Part   **Half**   **Most**   **Full**

Good deeds I did today

_ _ _ _ _ _ _ _ _ _ _ _ _ _ _ _ _ _ _

_ _ _ _ _ _ _ _ _ _ _ _ _ _ _ _ _ _ _

_ _ _ _ _ _ _ _ _ _ _ _ _ _ _ _ _ _ _

_ _ _ _ _ _ _ _ _ _ _ _ _ _ _ _ _ _ _

_ _ _ _ _ _ _ _ _ _ _ _ _ _ _ _ _ _ _

_ _ _ _ _ _ _ _ _ _ _ _ _ _ _ _ _ _ _

My Quran Tracker

Surah: _ _ _ _ _ _ _ _ _ _ _ _ _ _ _ _

Verse: _ _ _ _ _ _ _ _ To: _ _ _ _ _ _ _

What I'm Grateful For Today

♡

♡

♡

♡

♡

ight up your "Salah" journey by adding a pop of color to each one you performed today

Fajr	Duhr	Asr	Maghrib	Isha

What I accomplished today: _

_ _

_ _

How I felt: _

_ _

_ _

Word Search #1

Get your eyes and brains ready, because it's time to search for hidden words related to Ramadan! Can you find them all?

```
B Q B O X H O O K Q J
Y P D Q S I A U C E Q
A S Z D C S Q P V F O
B E R Q O E U D R I F
C C A M Z I R H Q P H
U P M O B D A L O I Z
T F A S T I N G W O A
B X D Q I F Q A K Q R
I P A U U T R E Y S E
C I N E U A Z O N A A
Z A K A T R U R Z F Z
```

Ramadan	Suhoor	Zakat
Fasting	Eid	Quran
Iftar	Mosque	Tarawih

Ramadan Maze Craze

Salat Duhr is here and the little boy needs your guiding hand to reach the mosque! Can you rise to the challenge and guide him?

Ramadan Day 2

My Fasting Today Was:

Part **Half** **Most** **Full**

Good deeds I did today

_____
_____
_____
_____
_____
_____
_____

My Quran Tracker

Surah: _ _ _ _ _ _ _ _ _ _ _ _ _ _

Verse: _ _ _ _ _ _ _ To: _ _ _ _ _ _

What I'm Grateful For Today

♥
♥
♥
♥
♥

Light up your "Salah" journey by adding a pop of color to each one you performed today

| Fajr | Duhr | Asr | Maghrib | Isha |

What I accomplished today: _____
_____
_____

How I felt: _____
_____
_____

6

Ramadan's Amazing Truths

Ramadan lasts for over a month and the date changes every year, but it always takes place during the ninth month of the Islamic calendar.

Did You Know?

Allah (SWT) imposed the fasting of Ramadan on Muslims in the second year of the Hijra and made it a pillar of Islam, and the Prophet Muhammad ﷺ fasted it nine times before his death.

There are two main meals in the month of Ramadan: Suhur and Iftar. Suhur is the morning meal before fasting, while Iftar is the meal to break the fast.

Did You Know?

Islam is based on five core principles or pillars, and fasting (sawm) is one of those five pillars. We fast as a means to reflect on our faith, learn self-discipline and empathise with those less fortunate.

Ramadan Day 3

My Fasting Today Was:

Part   **Half**   **Most**   **Full**

Good deeds I did today

_ _ _ _ _ _ _ _ _ _ _ _ _ _ _ _ _ _
_ _ _ _ _ _ _ _ _ _ _ _ _ _ _ _ _ _
_ _ _ _ _ _ _ _ _ _ _ _ _ _ _ _ _ _
_ _ _ _ _ _ _ _ _ _ _ _ _ _ _ _ _ _
_ _ _ _ _ _ _ _ _ _ _ _ _ _ _ _ _ _
_ _ _ _ _ _ _ _ _ _ _ _ _ _ _ _ _ _

My Quran Tracker

Surah: _ _ _ _ _ _ _ _ _ _ _ _ _ _ _

Verse: _ _ _ _ _ _ _ To: _ _ _ _ _ _

What I'm Grateful For Today

♥
♥
♥
♥
♥

ight up your "Salah" journey by adding a pop of color to each one you performed today

| Fajr | Duhr | Asr | Maghrib | Isha |

What I accomplished today: _

How I felt: _

Ramadan Drawing

Put your artistic talents to use by replicating the image with
your own drawing skills

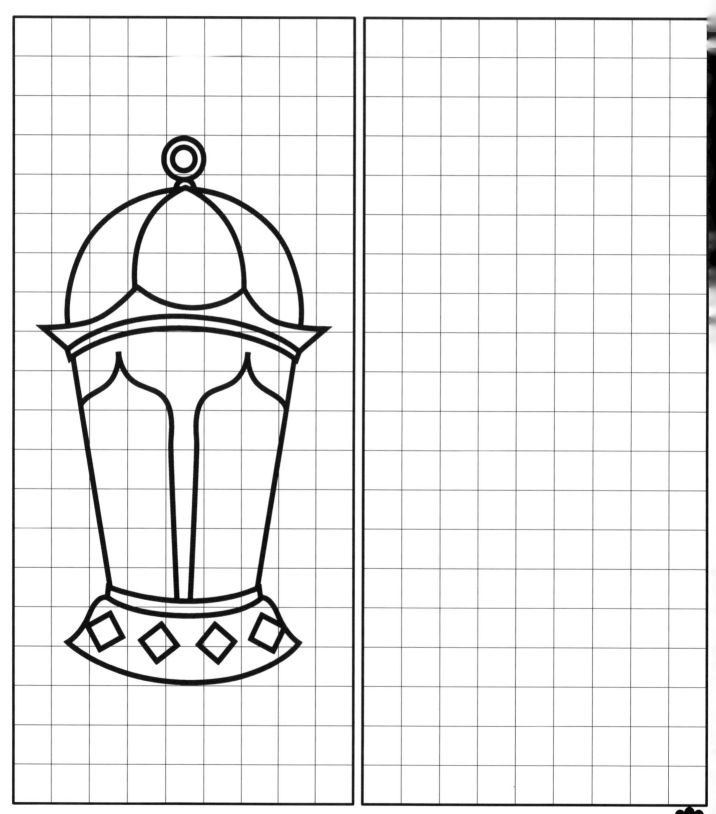

Create Your Own Sajadah

Unleash your inner designer! create a one-of-a-kind **Sajadah** for your loved ones

Ramadan Day 4

My Fasting Today Was:

Part   **Half**   **Most**   **Full**

Good deeds I did today

My Quran Tracker

Surah: _ _ _ _ _ _ _ _ _ _ _ _ _ _ _

Verse: _ _ _ _ _ _ _ To: _ _ _ _ _ _ _

What I'm Grateful For Today

♥ _____

♥ _____

♥ _____

♥ _____

♥ _____

Light up your "Salah" journey by adding a pop of color to each one you performed today

| Fajr | Duhr | Asr | Maghrib | Isha |

What I accomplished today: _

_ _

_ _

How I felt: _

_ _

_ _

Ramadan Acrostic Poem #1

An acrostic poem is a type of poem where the first letter of each line spells out a word or phrase. All lines should relate to or Describe the poem.
Write an acrostic poem for the word below

Ramadan

R _____

A _____

M _____

A _____

D _____

A _____

N _____

The Story Of Prophet Adam (AS)

In a distant time, Allah (SWT) created the universe in six days. He created the heavens, the earth, the planets, the stars and demonstrated his greatness in his creation. He made the earth we live on beautiful with mountains, rivers, oceans and various land and sea creatures.

Then Allah (SWT) wanted to create man, So Allah (SWT) created the first human, our father Adam (AS) peace be upon him. He was made from clay and given the most perfect appearance, then Allah (SWT) breathed life into him. After that, Allah (SWT) ordered the angels to bow down to Adam in respect and honor, and all the angels bowed down except for Iblis, who refused to bow down and defied Allah's (SWT) command and considered himself superior to Adam (AS). So Allah (SWT) cursed Iblis and expelled him from his mercy.

Then Allah (SWT) created a companion for our father Adam (AS), and that was his wife, Hawa. They lived in paradise and ate from it as they pleased. But Iblis always whispered to them to eat from the forbidden tree, which Allah (SWT) had warned them not to approach. Allah (SWT) had warned Adam (AS) and his wife Hawa about Iblis , who was their enemy.

Iblis tempted Adam (AS) and Hawa by promising them eternity if they ate from the forbidden tree. He swore by Allah (SWT) that he was telling the truth. They believed him and said that no one could swear by Allah (SWT) and lie. So they ate from the forbidden tree. Because of this, Allah (SWT) cast Adam (AS) and Hawa down to earth, where they faced poverty and hardship.

Adam (AS) and Hawa were deeply regretful and sought for forgiveness and redemption. Allah (SWT) forgave them.

Adam (AS) was the very first person on earth, and he was also the first prophet chosen by Allah (SWT). He spread the message of Allah (SWT) and lived a life full of obedience and devotion.

The lesson we learn from Adam's story is that even the best of us can make mistakes and we should always strive to follow Allah's (SWT) commands and stay away from temptations. When we do make mistakes, we should ask for Allah's (SWT) forgiveness and try to be better the next time.

Ramadan Day 5

My Fasting Today Was:

Part	Half	Most	Full

Good deeds I did today

_ _ _ _ _ _ _ _ _ _ _ _ _ _ _ _ _ _

_ _ _ _ _ _ _ _ _ _ _ _ _ _ _ _ _ _

_ _ _ _ _ _ _ _ _ _ _ _ _ _ _ _ _ _

_ _ _ _ _ _ _ _ _ _ _ _ _ _ _ _ _ _

_ _ _ _ _ _ _ _ _ _ _ _ _ _ _ _ _ _

_ _ _ _ _ _ _ _ _ _ _ _ _ _ _ _ _ _

My Quran Tracker

Surah: _ _ _ _ _ _ _ _ _ _ _ _ _ _

Verse: _ _ _ _ _ _ _ To: _ _ _ _ _ _

What I'm Grateful For Today

♥

♥

♥

♥

♥

Light up your "Salah" journey by adding a pop of color to each one you performed today

Fajr	Duhr	Asr	Maghrib	Isha

What I accomplished today: _ _ _ _ _ _ _ _ _ _ _ _ _ _ _ _

_ _

_ _

How I felt: _

_ _

_ _

Islamic Nations Anagrams #1

Unscramble the names of the islamic nations and test your knowledge of the islamic world

Coma or   (Africa)

_ _ _ _ _ _ _ _ _ _ _ _ _ _ _ _ _ _

Rain   (Asia)

_ _ _ _ _ _ _ _ _ _ _ _ _ _ _ _ _ _

Qiara   (Asia)

_ _ _ _ _ _ _ _ _ _ _ _ _ _ _ _ _ _

Carasia Dais   (Asia)

_ _ _ _ _ _ _ _ _ _ _ _ _ _ _ _ _ _

Sinatu   (Africa)

_ _ _ _ _ _ _ _ _ _ _ _ _ _ _ _ _ _

Labiy   (Africa)

_ _ _ _ _ _ _ _ _ _ _ _ _ _ _ _ _ _

Quran Quest

Get ready for an adventure! Join the little girl on a quest to find her Quran by following the path of numbers in order from 1-20

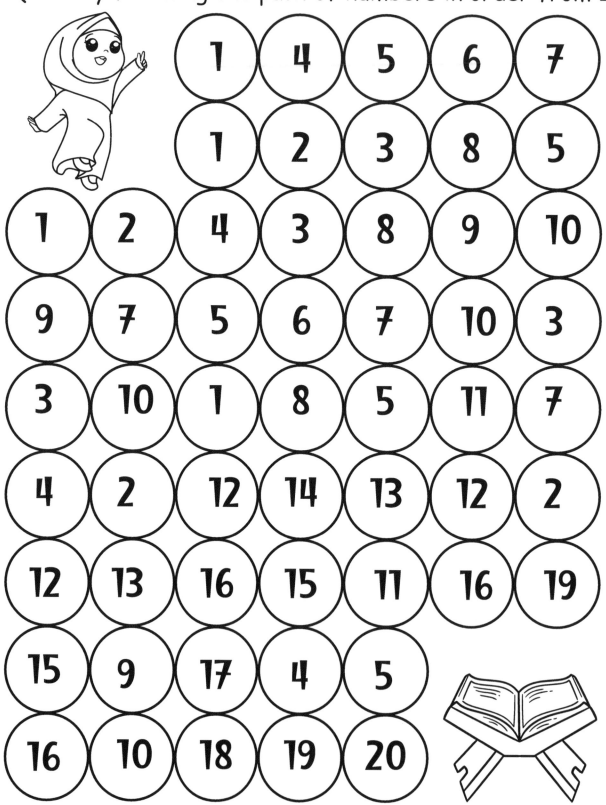

Ramadan Day 6

My Fasting Today Was:

Part   **Half**   **Most**   **Full**

Good deeds I did today

_ _ _ _ _ _ _ _ _ _ _ _ _ _ _ _ _ _ _ _

_ _ _ _ _ _ _ _ _ _ _ _ _ _ _ _ _ _ _ _

_ _ _ _ _ _ _ _ _ _ _ _ _ _ _ _ _ _ _ _

_ _ _ _ _ _ _ _ _ _ _ _ _ _ _ _ _ _ _ _

_ _ _ _ _ _ _ _ _ _ _ _ _ _ _ _ _ _ _ _

_ _ _ _ _ _ _ _ _ _ _ _ _ _ _ _ _ _ _ _

My Quran Tracker

Surah: _ _ _ _ _ _ _ _ _ _ _ _ _ _ _ _

Verse: _ _ _ _ _ _ _ To: _ _ _ _ _ _

What I'm Grateful For Today

Light up your "Salah" journey by adding a pop of color to each one you performed today

| Fajr | Duhr | Asr | Maghrib | Isha |

What I accomplished today: _

_ _

How I felt: _

_ _

Ramadan Crossword #1

Across

2. The fifth pillar of Islam

5. A pre-dawn meal consumed during Ramadan

7. The final prophet in Islam

10. The act of abstaining from food, drink, and other physical needs during daylight hours in Ramadan

Down

1. The second pillar of Islam

3. The act of giving to those in need during Ramadan

4. A celebration which follows the period of fasting

6. Holy month in Islam

8. An Islamic place of worship

9. A meal eaten after sunset during Ramadan to break the fast

Ramadan Coloring

Ramadan Day 7

My Fasting Today Was:

Part **Half** **Most** **Full**

Good deeds I did today

_ _ _ _ _ _ _ _ _ _ _ _ _ _ _

_ _ _ _ _ _ _ _ _ _ _ _ _ _ _

_ _ _ _ _ _ _ _ _ _ _ _ _ _ _

_ _ _ _ _ _ _ _ _ _ _ _ _ _ _

_ _ _ _ _ _ _ _ _ _ _ _ _ _ _

_ _ _ _ _ _ _ _ _ _ _ _ _ _ _

My Quran Tracker

Surah: _ _ _ _ _ _ _ _ _ _ _ _ _ _ _

Verse: _ _ _ _ _ _ _ To: _ _ _ _ _ _ _

What I'm Grateful For Today

♥

♥

♥

♥

♥

Light up your "Salah" journey by adding a pop of color to each one you performed today

| Fajr | Duhr | Asr | Maghrib | Isha |

What I accomplished today: _

_ _

_ _

How I felt: _

_ _

_ _

Word Search #2

Get your eyes and brains ready, because it's time to search for hidden words related to Ramadan! Can you find them all?

```
D  H  A  D  I  T  H  W  G  P  B
E  N  T  I  J  W  S  J  M  H  I
R  R  X  R  C  C  A  I  E  A  C
W  T  L  C  B  F  L  S  C  V  H
Z  Z  R  N  W  S  A  L  C  H  A
R  M  F  U  U  E  H  I  A  I  R
Q  W  O  M  D  G  I  Q  T  J  I
J  R  W  S  U  A  O  M  N  H  T
H  D  V  M  A  L  S  T  I  S  Y
E  I  D  A  L  F  I  T  R  I  Y
Z  R  F  L  P  R  A  Y  E  R  C
```

Hadith	Charity	Mecca
Salah	Eid al-Fitr	Muslim
Wudu	Prayer	Faith

The Five Pillars Of Islam

Join in on the fun and bring the Five Pillars of Islam to life as you recite and color them in with your imaginations!

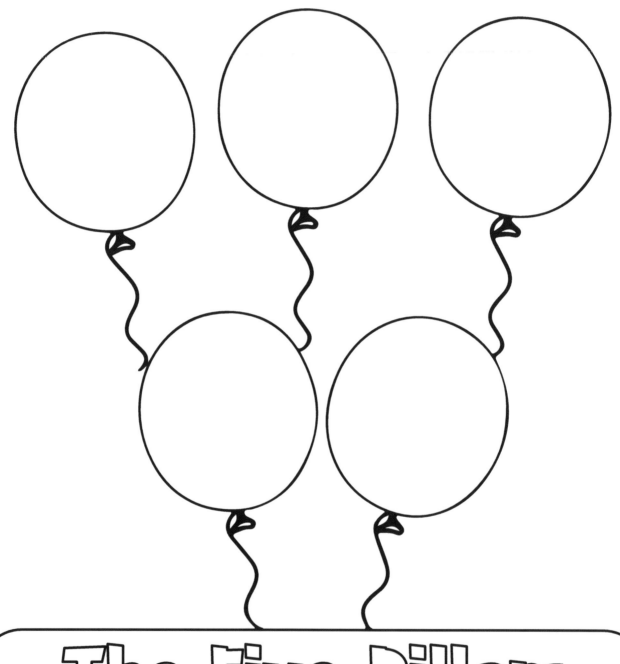

The Five Pillars Of Islam

Ramadan Day 8

My Fasting Today Was:

Part   **Half**   **Most**   **Full**

Good deeds I did today

_ _ _ _ _ _ _ _ _ _ _ _ _ _ _ _ _ _ _
_ _ _ _ _ _ _ _ _ _ _ _ _ _ _ _ _ _ _ _
_ _ _ _ _ _ _ _ _ _ _ _ _ _ _ _ _ _ _ _
_ _ _ _ _ _ _ _ _ _ _ _ _ _ _ _ _ _ _ _
_ _ _ _ _ _ _ _ _ _ _ _ _ _ _ _ _ _ _ _
_ _ _ _ _ _ _ _ _ _ _ _ _ _ _ _ _ _ _ _

My Quran Tracker

Surah: _ _ _ _ _ _ _ _ _ _ _ _ _ _ _ _

Verse: _ _ _ _ _ _ _ To: _ _ _ _ _ _

What I'm Grateful For Today

Light up your "Salah" journey by adding a pop of color to each one you performed today

| Fajr | Duhr | Asr | Maghrib | Isha |

What I accomplished today: _ _ _ _ _ _ _ _ _ _ _ _ _ _
_ _
_ _

How I felt: _
_ _
_ _

Hajj Maze

The Little Boy is Set to Embark on His Hajj Journey to Mecca, Can You Help Him Reach His Destination?

Ramadan's Amazing Truths

One of the most beautiful acts of worship during Ramadan is Salat Tarawih, which is a voluntary prayer performed during Ramadan starting after Al-Isha until dawn

Did You Know?

Laylat-al-Qadr, is the holiest eve in the Islamic calendar. It falls within the last 10 days of Ramadan and it's the night that the first verses of the Quran were given to the prophet Muhammed ﷺ by the angel Jibril

Not everyone is required to fast during Ramadan, including young children, the elderly, travelers, and the sick or pregnant woman if fasting poses a threat to their health

Did You Know?

Many Muslims break their fast for the day with dates as the prophet Muhammed was quoted saying, When one of you is fasting, he should break his fast with dates; but if he cannot get any, then (he should break his fast) with water, for water is purifying

Ramadan Scramble Game #1

Look at the letters around the picture.
Try to rearrange them to fill in the blanks

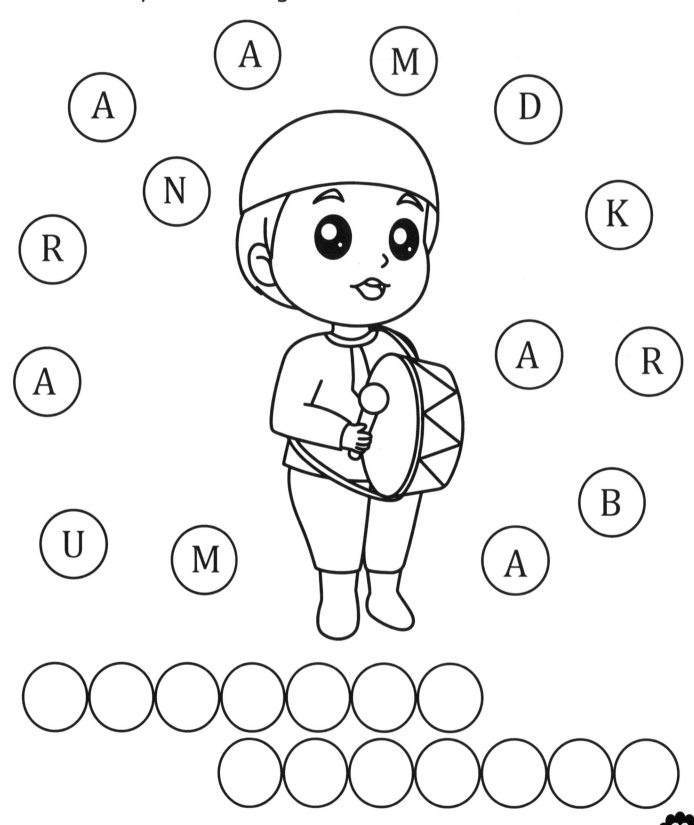

Ramadan Day 9

My Fasting Today Was:

Part	Half	Most	Full

Good deeds I did today

_ _

_ _

_ _

_ _

_ _

_ _

My Quran Tracker

Surah: _ _ _ _ _ _ _ _ _ _ _ _ _ _ _ _ _

Verse: _ _ _ _ _ _ _ To: _ _ _ _ _ _

What I'm Grateful For Today

-
-
-
-
-

Light up your "Salah" journey by adding a pop of color to each one you performed today

Fajr	Duhr	Asr	Maghrib	Isha

What I accomplished today: _

How I felt: _

Lantern Counting Activity

Let's count together! Keep track of the Lanterns and fill in the blank

🌙🌙🌙 + 🌙🌙 = ☐

🌙 + = 2

🌙🌙 + 🌙🌙🌙🌙🌙 = ☐

🌙🌙🌙🌙 + = 9

🌙 + 🌙🌙🌙 = ☐

🌙🌙🌙 + 🌙🌙🌙 = ☐

🌙🌙🌙🌙 + = 8

🌙 + 🌙🌙 = ☐

30

Ramadan Drawing

Put your artistic talents to use by replicating the image with your own drawing skills

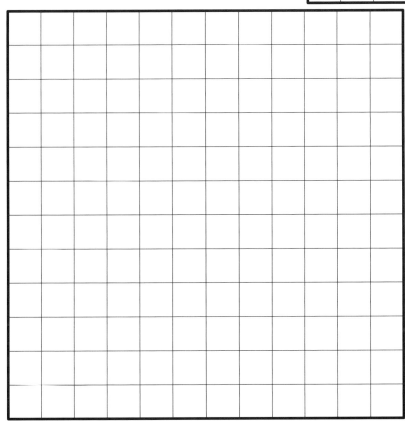

Ramadan Day 10

My Fasting Today Was:

Part   **Half**   **Most**   **Full**

Good deeds I did today

_____
_____
_____
_____
_____
_____
_____

My Quran Tracker

Surah: _ _ _ _ _ _ _ _ _ _ _ _ _ _ _ _ _

Verse: _ _ _ _ _ _ _ To: _ _ _ _ _ _ _

What I'm Grateful For Today

♥
♥
♥
♥
♥

Light up your "Salah" journey by adding a pop of color to each one you performed today

Fajr	Duhr	Asr	Maghrib	Isha

What I accomplished today: _____
_____
_____

How I felt: _____
_____
_____

Ramadan Doodles

Express your love for Ramadan with your doodles! Grab your pen or pencil and let your imagination run wild as you create fun and colorful drawings inspired by the holy month

Ramadan Acrostic Poem #2

An acrostic poem is a type of poem where the first letter of each line spells out a word or phrase. All lines should relate to or Describe the poem.

Write an acrostic poem for the word below

Salat

S _____

A _____

L _____

A _____

T _____

Ramadan Day 11

My Fasting Today Was:

Part	Half	Most	Full

Good deeds I did today

_ _

_ _

_ _

_ _

_ _

_ _

_ _

My Quran Tracker

Surah: _ _ _ _ _ _ _ _ _ _ _ _ _ _ _ _

Verse: _ _ _ _ _ _ _ To: _ _ _ _ _ _

What I'm Grateful For Today

♡ _____

♡ _____

♡ _____

♡ _____

♡ _____

Light up your "Salah" journey by adding a pop of color to each one you performed today

Fajr	Duhr	Asr	Maghrib	Isha

What I accomplished today: _ _ _ _ _ _ _ _ _ _ _ _ _ _ _ _ _ _ _

_ _

_ _

How I felt: _

_ _

_ _

Create Your Own Lantern

Get creative with light and color! Design your own unique lantern to light up the night during Ramadan

Islamic Nations Anagrams #2

Unscramble the names of the islamic nations and test your
knowledge of the islamic world

Rayis (Asia)

_ _ _ _ _ _ _ _ _ _ _ _ _ _ _ _ _ _ _ _

Exgyt (Africa)

_ _ _ _ _ _ _ _ _ _ _ _ _ _ _ _ _ _ _ _

Mano (Asia)

_ _ _ _ _ _ _ _ _ _ _ _ _ _ _ _ _ _ _ _

Aneleasti Ma Drubu (Asia)

_ _ _ _ _ _ _ _ _ _ _ _ _ _ _ _ _ _ _ _

Nemye (Asia)

_ _ _ _ _ _ _ _ _ _ _ _ _ _ _ _ _ _ _ _

Ahabirn (Asia)

_ _ _ _ _ _ _ _ _ _ _ _ _ _ _ _ _ _ _ _

Ramadan Day 12

My Fasting Today Was:

Part	Half	Most	Full

Good deeds I did today

_ _ _ _ _ _ _ _ _ _ _ _ _ _ _ _ _ _ _ _

_ _

_ _

_ _

_ _

_ _

_ _

My Quran Tracker

Surah: _ _ _ _ _ _ _ _ _ _ _ _ _ _ _ _ _ _

Verse: _ _ _ _ _ _ _ To: _ _ _ _ _ _ _

What I'm Grateful For Today

♡

♡

♡

♡

♡

Light up your "Salah" journey by adding a pop of color to each one you performed today

Fajr	Duhr	Asr	Maghrib	Isha

What I accomplished today: _

_ _

_ _

How I felt: _

_ _

_ _

Ramadan Crossword #2

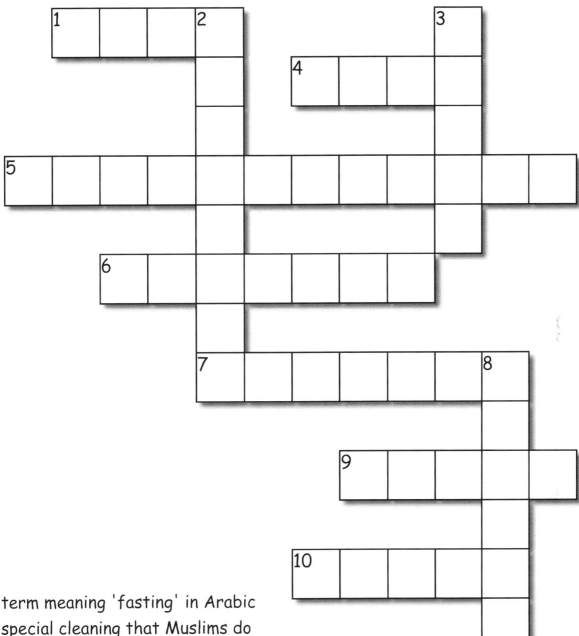

Across

1. A term meaning 'fasting' in Arabic

4. A special cleaning that Muslims do before praying

5. The night when the first verses of the Quran were revealed to the Prophet Muhammad

6. A voluntary (nafl) night prayer performed only in Ramadan

7. Believers of islam faith

9. Muslim call to prayer

10. islam's holiest city

Down

2. The first month of the Islamic calendar

3. Islamic holy book

8. The month that comes before Ramadan

The Story Of Prophet Yunus (AS)

Yunus (AS) was a prophet chosen by Allah (SWT) to teach the people of Nineveh, a city that had gone astray. Despite his efforts to show the people the right path, they refused to listen. Dejected, Yunus boarded a ship and sailed far away.

But disaster struck when a massive storm hit the ship and threatened to sink it. The passengers were afraid they would drown and made a bold decision. They would draw lots to see who would be thrown overboard to save the rest. Three times, the lot fell on Yunus (AS), and he was cast into the sea.

But Allah (SWT) had other plans. He sent a giant whale, to swallow Yunus (AS) whole. Yunus (AS) was plunged into darkness. But even in his deepest despair, Yunus cried out to Allah (SWT) for help. And Allah, the Most Merciful, heard him.

With Allah's (SWT) guidance, Yunus (AS) realized that he was not in control and proclaimed "there is no god but You." This sincere act of repentance moved Allah (SWT) deeply, and He commanded the fish to release Yunus (AS) on the nearest shore. Yunus (AS) emerged from the fish's belly, his body inflamed from the acids, but Allah (SWT) provided for him. He made a tree grow to provide Yunus (AS) with food and shade.

Fully recovered, Yunus (AS) returned to Nineveh to complete his mission. To his amazement, the entire population had accepted Islam and was eagerly waiting for him. With his people, Yunus (AS) prostrated to Allah (SWT) and thanked Him for all His blessings.

The lesson we learn from the story of Yunus (AS) is the importance of seeking help from Allah (SWT) during difficult times and having faith in His mercy and control over all things.

Ramadan Day 13

My Fasting Today Was:

Part **Half** **Most** **Full**

Good deeds I did today

_ _ _ _ _ _ _ _ _ _ _ _ _ _ _ _ _ _ _

_ _ _ _ _ _ _ _ _ _ _ _ _ _ _ _ _ _ _

_ _ _ _ _ _ _ _ _ _ _ _ _ _ _ _ _ _ _

_ _ _ _ _ _ _ _ _ _ _ _ _ _ _ _ _ _ _

_ _ _ _ _ _ _ _ _ _ _ _ _ _ _ _ _ _ _

_ _ _ _ _ _ _ _ _ _ _ _ _ _ _ _ _ _ _

_ _ _ _ _ _ _ _ _ _ _ _ _ _ _ _ _ _ _

My Quran Tracker

Surah: _ _ _ _ _ _ _ _ _ _ _ _ _ _ _ _

Verse: _ _ _ _ _ _ _ To: _ _ _ _ _ _

What I'm Grateful For Today

♥

♥

♥

♥

♥

Light up your "Salah" journey by adding a pop of color to each one you performed today

Fajr	Duhr	Asr	Maghrib	Isha

What I accomplished today: _

How I felt: _

Ramadan Coloring

Word Search #3

Get your eyes and brains ready, because it's time to search for hidden words related to Ramadan! Can you find them all?

```
E  I  D  A  L  A  D  H  A  D  X
P  C  C  I  V  B  C  G  I  Y  H
B  G  S  S  L  X  J  J  F  I  T
N  F  I  L  Z  G  S  E  W  E  B
W  S  H  A  H  A  D  A  S  A  N
I  L  I  M  M  N  R  I  W  W  X
C  U  J  H  K  A  D  L  Y  I  V
M  M  A  W  T  A  O  S  P  P  I
Q  U  B  P  R  O  P  H  E  T  W
D  Y  H  A  D  I  T  H  U  M  H
Q  K  P  A  F  V  O  T  U  K  F
```

Eid Al-adha   Dua   Shahada

Prophet   Masjid   Paradise

Islam   Hijab   Tarawih

Ramadan Day 14

My Fasting Today Was:

Part   Half   Most   Full

Good deeds I did today

_ _

_ _

_ _

_ _

_ _

_ _

My Quran Tracker

Surah: _ _ _ _ _ _ _ _ _ _ _ _ _ _ _ _

Verse: _ _ _ _ _ _ _ To: _ _ _ _ _ _

What I'm Grateful For Today

Light up your "Salah" journey by adding a pop of color to each one you performed today

| Fajr | Duhr | Asr | Maghrib | Isha |

What I accomplished today: _

_ _

_ _

How I felt: _

_ _

_ _

Ramadan Greeting Card

Get ready to spread love and joy with your very own Ramadan Greeting Card! Use your creativity and imagination to design a special card for your family and friends to show how much you care

A Journey Through Ramadan

Take on a thrilling challenge as you navigate through the Ramadan Maze in search of your delicious Iftar meal!

Ramadan Day 15

My Fasting Today Was:

Part	Half	Most	Full

Good deeds I did today

_____
_____
_____
_____
_____
_____
_____

My Quran Tracker

Surah: _____

Verse: _____ To: _____

What I'm Grateful For Today

♥

♥

♥

♥

♥

Light up your "Salah" journey by adding a pop of color to each one you performed today

Fajr	Duhr	Asr	Maghrib	Isha

What I accomplished today: _____
_____
_____

How I felt: _____
_____
_____

48

Halfway Through Ramadan

Unleash your thoughts on the journey of the first half of Ramadan - share your fasting experiences, the ups and downs, and what you've learned. Reveal your favorite Iftar meal and set your goals for the rest of the holy month with purpose and intention

- -

- -

- -

- -

- -

- -

- -

- -

- -

- -

- -

- -

- -

- -

- -

Salah Sky Draw

Draw the sky during the time of each salah

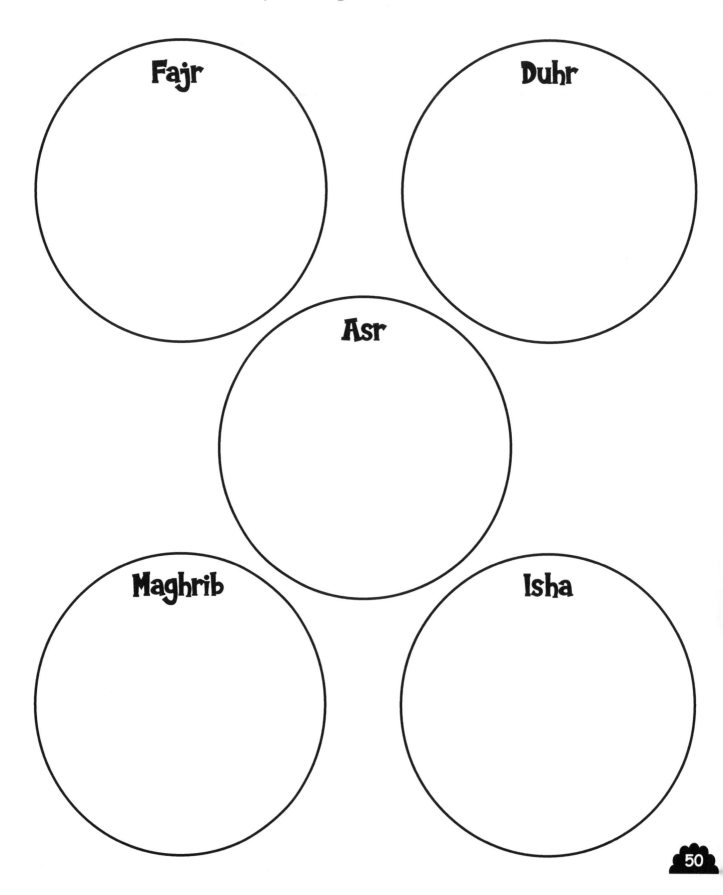

Fajr

Duhr

Asr

Maghrib

Isha

Ramadan Day 16

My Fasting Today Was:

Part   Half   Most   Full

Good deeds I did today

_ _ _ _ _ _ _ _ _ _ _ _ _ _ _ _ _ _ _ _

_ _

_ _

_ _

_ _

_ _

My Quran Tracker

Surah: _ _ _ _ _ _ _ _ _ _ _ _ _ _ _ _

Verse: _ _ _ _ _ _ _ To: _ _ _ _ _ _ _

What I'm Grateful For Today

♡

♡

♡

♡

♡

Light up your "Salah" journey by adding a pop of color to each one you performed today

Fajr	Duhr	Asr	Maghrib	Isha

What I accomplished today: _ _ _ _ _ _ _ _ _ _ _ _ _ _ _ _ _ _

_ _

_ _

How I felt: _

_ _

_ _

Islamic Months

Order Up! Can You Put the Islamic Months in the Correct Sequence?

Dhū al-Hijjah	Safar	Jumādā al-Thānī	Rabīʿ al-Thānī
Dhū al-Qaʿdah	Rajab	Rabīʿ al-Awwal	Muharram
Shawwāl	Shaʿbān	Jumādā al-Awwal	Ramadān

1. _____

2. _____

3. _____

4. _____

5. _____

6. _____

7. _____

8. _____

9. _____

10. _____

11. _____

12. _____

Ramadan Scramble Game #2

Look at the letters around the picture.
Try to rearrange them to fill in the blanks

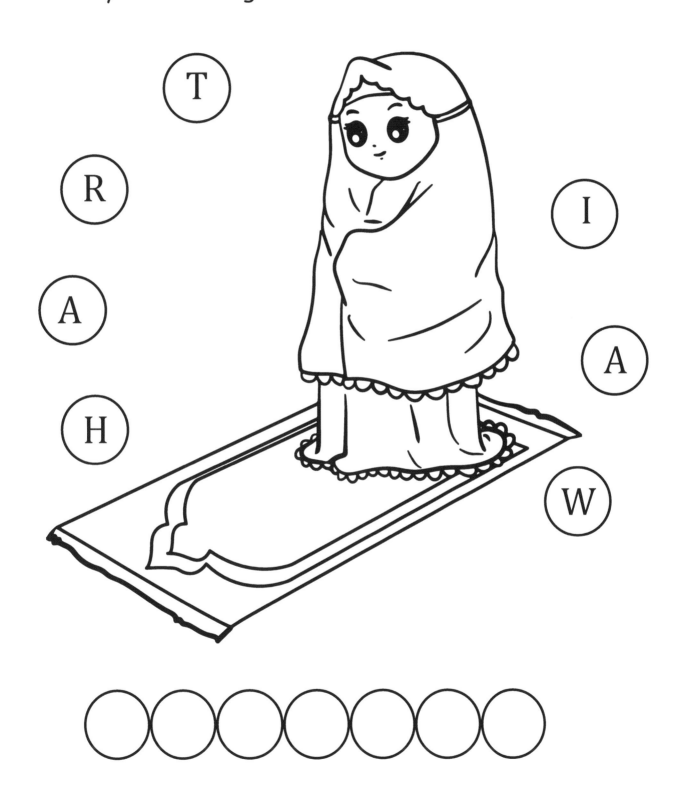

Ramadan Day 17

My Fasting Today Was:

Part   **Half**   **Most**   **Full**

Good deeds I did today

_ _ _ _ _ _ _ _ _ _ _ _ _ _ _ _ _
_ _ _ _ _ _ _ _ _ _ _ _ _ _ _ _ _
_ _ _ _ _ _ _ _ _ _ _ _ _ _ _ _ _
_ _ _ _ _ _ _ _ _ _ _ _ _ _ _ _ _
_ _ _ _ _ _ _ _ _ _ _ _ _ _ _ _ _
_ _ _ _ _ _ _ _ _ _ _ _ _ _ _ _ _
_ _ _ _ _ _ _ _ _ _ _ _ _ _ _ _ _

My Quran Tracker

Surah: _ _ _ _ _ _ _ _ _ _ _ _ _ _

Verse: _ _ _ _ _ _ _ To: _ _ _ _ _ _

What I'm Grateful For Today

♥
♥
♥
♥
♥

Light up your "Salah" journey by adding a pop of color to each one you performed today

| Fajr | Duhr | Asr | Maghrib | Isha |

What I accomplished today: _
_ _
_ _

How I felt: _
_ _
_ _

Ramadan Drawing

Mirror the image! Finish the right side of the picture
by copying the lines from the left side

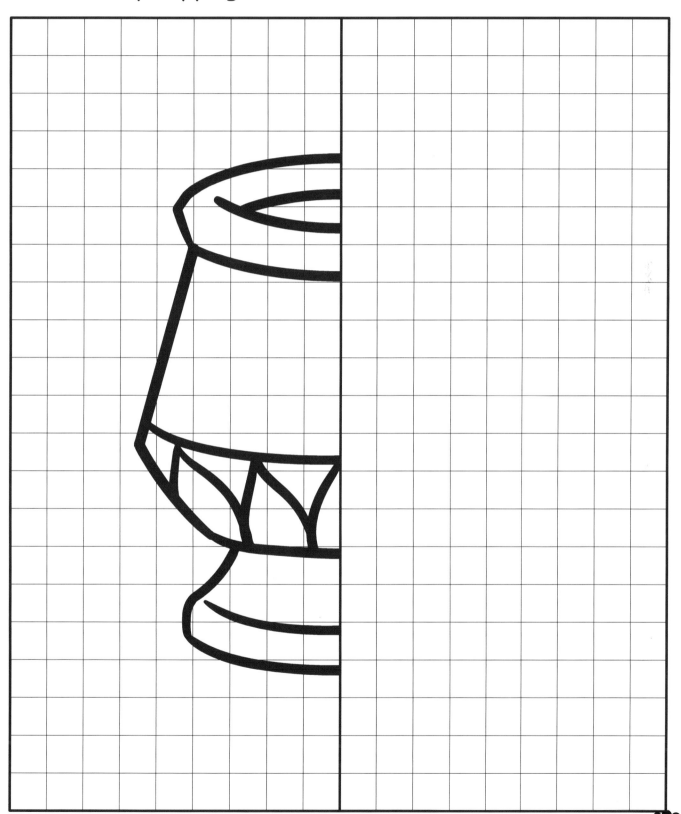

Odd and Even Sajadah

Can you color the EVEN numbered Sajadah?

7

15

10

99

18

36

45

19

20

37

88

80

1

24

Ramadan Day 18

My Fasting Today Was:

Part Half Most Full

Good deeds I did today

_ _

_ _

_ _

_ _

_ _

_ _

_ _

My Quran Tracker

Surah: _ _ _ _ _ _ _ _ _ _ _ _ _ _ _ _

Verse: _ _ _ _ _ _ _ To: _ _ _ _ _ _ _

What I'm Grateful For Today

♥

♥

♥

♥

♥

Light up your "Salah" journey by adding a pop of color to each one you performed today

| Fajr | Duhr | Asr | Maghrib | Isha |

What I accomplished today: _

_ _

_ _

How I felt: _

_ _

_ _

Connect The Dots #1

Join the fun! Connect the dots from 1 to 102 and discover the hidden picture

Muslim Festivals

Get ready to put your knowledge to the test! read the statements carefully, and pick the correct answer from the list above

Eid al-Fitr	Eid al-Adha	Ramadan
Maulid Al-Nabi	Muharram	Lyalat al-Qadr

Ninth month in the Islamic calendar, devoted to fasting, prayer, and reflection

Marks the end of the month-long fasting period.

Commemorates the birth of Prophet Muhammad

Celebrated in memory of Prophet Ibrahim's willingness to sacrifice his son for Allah

The night that the first verses of the Quran were revealed to Prophet Muhammad.

Ramadan Day 19

My Fasting Today Was:

Part   Half   Most   Full

Good deeds
I did today

_ _ _ _ _ _ _ _ _ _ _ _ _
_ _ _ _ _ _ _ _ _ _ _ _ _
_ _ _ _ _ _ _ _ _ _ _ _ _
_ _ _ _ _ _ _ _ _ _ _ _ _
_ _ _ _ _ _ _ _ _ _ _ _ _
_ _ _ _ _ _ _ _ _ _ _ _ _
_ _ _ _ _ _ _ _ _ _ _ _ _

My Quran Tracker

Surah: _ _ _ _ _ _ _ _ _ _ _ _ _ _ _

Verse: _ _ _ _ _ _ _ To: _ _ _ _ _ _

What I'm Grateful For Today

♥
♥
♥
♥
♥

Light up your "Salah" journey by adding a pop
of color to each one you performed today

| Fajr | Duhr | Asr | Maghrib | Isha |

What I accomplished today: _
_ _
_ _

How I felt: _
_ _
_ _

Iftar Meal

Special Dua before breaking the fast

"اللهم لكَ صُمت وعلى رزقك أفطرت، ذهب الظمأ وابتلت العروق وثبت الأجر إن شاء الله"

Draw and Color the yummiest dish you'd love to have during iftar time!

Ramadan Acrostic Poem #3

An acrostic poem is a type of poem where the first letter of each line spells out a word or phrase. All lines should relate to or Describe the poem.

Write an acrostic poem for the word below

Sawm

S _____

A _____

W _____

M _____

Ramadan Day 20

My Fasting Today Was:

Part **Half** **Most** **Full**

Good deeds I did today

My Quran Tracker

Surah: _ _ _ _ _ _ _ _ _ _ _ _ _ _ _

Verse: _ _ _ _ _ _ _ To: _ _ _ _ _ _ _

What I'm Grateful For Today

♥

♥

♥

♥

♥

Light up your "Salah" journey by adding a pop of color to each one you performed today

Fajr	Duhr	Asr	Maghrib	Isha

What I accomplished today: _____

How I felt: _____

Ramadan Math #1

Time to show off your math skills! Help the little boy find his way to the masjid by coloring only the circles that have even numbers inside!

54 x 5 =

37 x 3 =

85 x 7 =

53 x 9 =

26 x 6 =

86 x 9 =

48 x 2 =

27 x 7 =

87 x 3 =

79 x 5 =

37 x 8 =

88 x 7 =

75 x 6 =

64 x 4 =

98 x 3 =

96 x 5 =

47 x 9 =

Ramadan's Amazing Truths

Muslims read the whole Qur'an, at least once, during Ramadan, and special services take place at mosques where the Qur'an is read.

Did You Know?

Ramadan concludes with Eid al-Fitr, a celebration which follows the period of fasting. It is a day of joy and thanking Allah(SWT) for the strength in accomplishing the spiritual month. It is a day of gratitude, prayers, unity and happiness

More than 1.6 billion Muslims across the globe celebrate Ramadan, with charity being an important part of the celebration Giving to charity voluntarily is known as "Sadaqa"

Did You Know?

Ramadan is announced every year based on the sighting of the crescent moon. The sighting of the Ramadan crescent begins on the 29th of Sha'ban, and if it is confirmed, the next day is the first day of Ramadan. If it is not confirmed, the next day is the completion of the month of Sha'ban.

Ramadan Day 21

My Fasting Today Was:

Part   Half   Most   Full

Good deeds I did today

- - - - - - - - - - - - - - - - - - -
- - - - - - - - - - - - - - - - - - -
- - - - - - - - - - - - - - - - - - -
- - - - - - - - - - - - - - - - - - -
- - - - - - - - - - - - - - - - - - -
- - - - - - - - - - - - - - - - - - -
- - - - - - - - - - - - - - - - - - -

My Quran Tracker

Surah: - - - - - - - - - - - - - - -

Verse: - - - - - - - - To: - - - - - - -

What I'm Grateful For Today

♥
♥
♥
♥
♥

Light up your "Salah" journey by adding a pop of color to each one you performed today

Fajr	Duhr	Asr	Maghrib	Isha

What I accomplished today: - - - - - - - - - - - - - - - - - -
- -
- -

How I felt: -
- -
- -

Ramadan Coloring

Prophets Names

Put your Islamic knowledge to the test! How many prophets can you name?

1. _____   2. _____

3. _____   4. _____

5. _____   6. _____

7. _____   8. _____

9. _____   10. _____

11. _____   12. _____

13. _____   14. _____

15. _____   16. _____

17. _____   18. _____

19. _____   20. _____

Ramadan Day 22

My Fasting Today Was:

Part	Half	Most	Full

Good deeds I did today

_ _ _ _ _ _ _ _ _ _ _ _ _ _ _ _ _ _ _ _
_ _ _ _ _ _ _ _ _ _ _ _ _ _ _ _ _ _ _ _
_ _ _ _ _ _ _ _ _ _ _ _ _ _ _ _ _ _ _ _
_ _ _ _ _ _ _ _ _ _ _ _ _ _ _ _ _ _ _ _
_ _ _ _ _ _ _ _ _ _ _ _ _ _ _ _ _ _ _ _
_ _ _ _ _ _ _ _ _ _ _ _ _ _ _ _ _ _ _ _

My Quran Tracker

Surah: _ _ _ _ _ _ _ _ _ _ _ _ _ _ _ _ _

Verse: _ _ _ _ _ _ _ To: _ _ _ _ _ _ _

What I'm Grateful For Today

♥
♥
♥
♥
♥

Light up your "Salah" journey by adding a pop of color to each one you performed today

Fajr	Duhr	Asr	Maghrib	Isha

What I accomplished today: _

How I felt: _

The Story Of Prophet Nuh (AS)

Long after Prophet Adam (pbuh), people strayed from worshiping Allah (SWT) and instead began praying to idols. They relied on the assistance of these idol statues instead of seeking help from Allah (SWT).

Prophet Nuh (pbuh) was sent by Allah (SWT) to educate his people on the dangers of idol worship and to instruct them to only pray to Allah (SWT). Prophet Nuh (pbuh) was an effective communicator and a patient man, but despite his efforts, only a few followed his teachings.

The majority of people did not listen and even became angry with Prophet Nuh (pbuh). He warned them that their actions would result in punishment from Allah, but they disregarded his warnings and covered their ears to avoid hearing his words.

Prophet Nuh (pbuh) tried for 950 years to guide his people, but to no avail. Allah (SWT) informed Prophet Nuh (pbuh) that no one else would believe and so he prayed for their destruction.

As per Allah's (SWT) command, Prophet Nuh (pbuh) built a ship with Allah's (SWT) guidance. His people mocked him for building a ship on land, but he persevered and completed the construction with Allah's (SWT) help.

When the sign from Allah (SWT) came, Prophet Nuh (pbuh) loaded the ship with his followers and a pair of every kind of animal, bird, and insect. A great flood was sent by Allah (SWT) to punish those who did not listen to Prophet Nuh (pbuh) and only those in the ship survived.

The flood eventually subsided, and the ship landed on Mount Judiyy. Prophet Nuh (pbuh) released all the animals and thanked Allah (SWT) for their salvation.

And from that day on, Prophet Nuh (pbuh) became a guide to his people and taught them how to live a righteous life, always worshiping Allah (SWT) alone.

Word Search #4

Get your eyes and brains ready, because it's time to search for hidden prophets names! Can you find them all?

```
F  D  N  L  O  I  E  A  I  Y  U
L  M  U  H  A  M  M  A  D  V  S
S  I  H  M  V  U  R  E  R  A  Y
P  Z  Z  I  B  R  A  H  I  M  M
V  M  P  T  F  B  A  U  S  R  U
F  W  K  W  F  I  A  A  X  A  S
S  I  M  U  S  A  S  R  N  F  S
L  A  S  U  L  A  Y  M  A  N  V
F  U  I  N  N  X  G  I  A  Y  Y
Y  P  Z  W  T  Q  D  Y  N  I  M
B  Z  U  Q  H  X  W  H  Q  D  L
```

Adam	Ibrahim	Sulayman
Idris	Yusuf	Muhammad
Nuh	Musa	Ismail

Ramadan Day 23

My Fasting Today Was:

Part   Half   Most   Full

Good deeds I did today

_ _ _ _ _ _ _ _ _ _ _ _ _ _ _ _ _ _

_ _ _ _ _ _ _ _ _ _ _ _ _ _ _ _ _ _

_ _ _ _ _ _ _ _ _ _ _ _ _ _ _ _ _ _

_ _ _ _ _ _ _ _ _ _ _ _ _ _ _ _ _ _

_ _ _ _ _ _ _ _ _ _ _ _ _ _ _ _ _ _

_ _ _ _ _ _ _ _ _ _ _ _ _ _ _ _ _ _

_ _ _ _ _ _ _ _ _ _ _ _ _ _ _ _ _ _

My Quran Tracker

Surah: _ _ _ _ _ _ _ _ _ _ _ _ _ _ _

Verse: _ _ _ _ _ _ _ To: _ _ _ _ _ _ _

What I'm Grateful For Today

♥

♥

♥

♥

♥

Light up your "Salah" journey by adding a pop of color to each one you performed today

| Fajr | Duhr | Asr | Maghrib | Isha |

What I accomplished today: _

_ _

_ _

How I felt: _

_ _

_ _

Connect The Dots #2

Join the fun! Connect the dots from 1 to 44 and discover the hidden picture

Ramadan Crossword #3

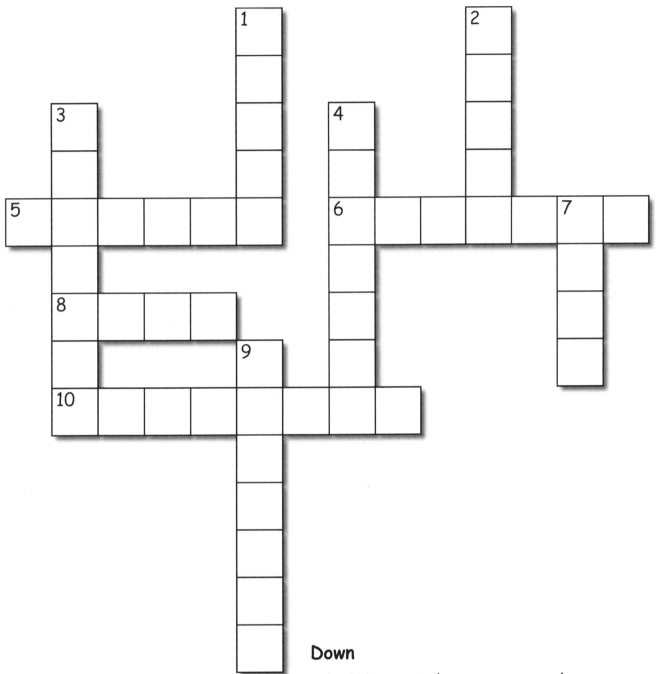

Across

5. lantern in arabic

6. Known as the father of all prophets

8. The first word revealed to muhammad (pbuh)

10. The first caliph of Islam

Down

1. We must do as many good .... as we can

2. Where was the prophet muhammad (pbuh) born

3. first wife of prophet muhammad (pbuh)

4. The first pillar of Islam

7. The first human being ever created

9. Sunset time

Ramadan Day 24

My Fasting Today Was:

Part	Half	Most	Full

Good deeds I did today

_____
_____
_____
_____
_____
_____
_____

My Quran Tracker

Surah: _____

Verse: _____ To: _____

What I'm Grateful For Today

♥ _____

♥ _____

♥ _____

♥ _____

♥ _____

Light up your "Salah" journey by adding a pop of color to each one you performed today

Fajr	Duhr	Asr	Maghrib	Isha

What I accomplished today: _____
_____
_____

How I felt: _____
_____
_____

Noor's Sajadah Search

Noor's in a pickle! She's ready for Salat al-Asr, but her Sajadah's gone missing. Can you lend a hand and help her find it?

Ramadan Math #2

Put your math skills to the test and find the value of each?

🧺 + 🕌 = 🌙⭐ + 1

☕ + ☕ = 🧺

5 = ☕ + 🌙⭐

🌙⭐ − 3 = 1

🧺 = ☐   🕌 = ☐   🌙⭐ = ☐

☕ = ☐

Ramadan Day 25

My Fasting Today Was:

Part   Half   Most   Full

Good deeds I did today

_____

_____

_____

_____

_____

_____

_____

My Quran Tracker

Surah: _ _ _ _ _ _ _ _ _ _ _ _ _ _ _

Verse: _ _ _ _ _ _ _ To: _ _ _ _ _ _ _

What I'm Grateful For Today

♡

♡

♡

♡

♡

Light up your "Salah" journey by adding a pop of color to each one you performed today

Fajr	Duhr	Asr	Maghrib	Isha

What I accomplished today: _____

_____

_____

How I felt: _____

_____

_____

Islamic Nations Anagrams #3

Unscramble the names of the islamic nations and test your knowledge of the islamic world

Agrlei   (Africa)

- - - - - - - - - - - - - - - - - -

Bneonla   (Asia)

- - - - - - - - - - - - - - - - - -

Sandu   (Africa)

- - - - - - - - - - - - - - - - - -

Donjar   (Asia)

- - - - - - - - - - - - - - - - - -

Twuak   (Asia)

- - - - - - - - - - - - - - - - - -

Tqara   (Asia)

- - - - - - - - - - - - - - - - - -

Ramadan Drawing

Mirror the image! Finish the right side of the picture by copying the lines from the left side

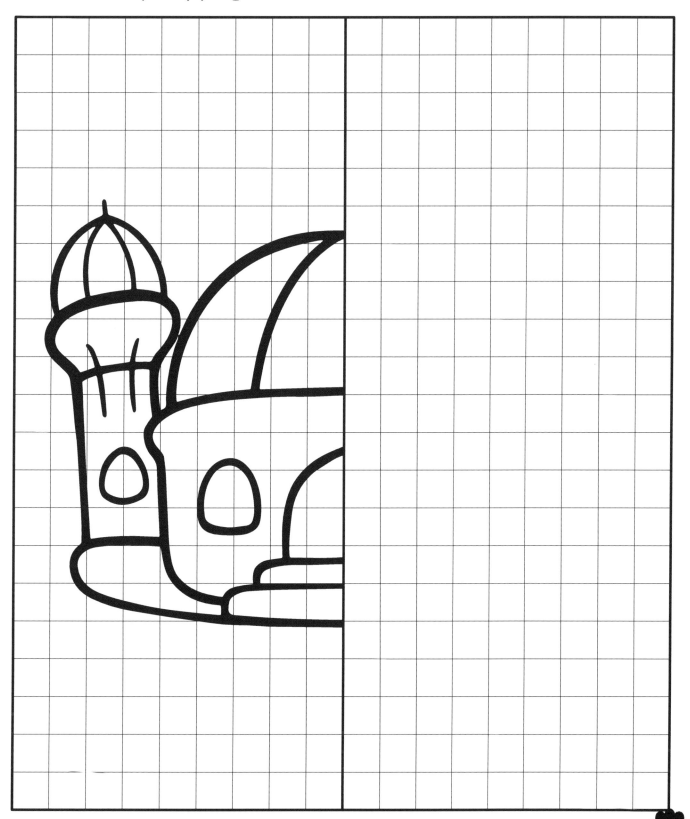

81

Ramadan Day 26

My Fasting Today Was:

Part **Half** **Most** **Full**

Good deeds
I did today

- -
- -
- -
- -
- -
- -
- -

My Quran Tracker

Surah: _ _ _ _ _ _ _ _ _ _ _ _ _ _ _

Verse: _ _ _ _ _ _ _   To: _ _ _ _ _ _

What I'm Grateful For Today

♥
♥
♥
♥
♥

Light up your "Salah" journey by adding a pop
of color to each one you performed today

| Fajr | Duhr | Asr | Maghrib | Isha |

What I accomplished today:

- -
- -
- -

How I felt:

- -
- -
- -

Ramadan Coloring

Ramadan's Amazing Truths

Did You Know?

Eid al-Fitr is a time for Muslims to wear their best outfits and dress to impress!

Muslims only eat food that is halal, this means that pork is forbidden along with drinking alcohol.

The dates of Ramadan can change by around 11 days each year because of the Lunar calendar.

Did You Know?

Did you know that there are over 1.9 billion people in the world who follow the religion of Islam? That's a lot of people! They come from different countries and cultures, but they all believe in Allah (SWT) and follow the teachings of the Prophet Muhammad ﷺ

Ramadan Day 27

My Fasting Today Was:

Part   Half   Most   Full

Good deeds I did today

_ _ _ _ _ _ _ _ _ _ _ _ _ _ _ _ _

_ _ _ _ _ _ _ _ _ _ _ _ _ _ _ _ _

_ _ _ _ _ _ _ _ _ _ _ _ _ _ _ _ _

_ _ _ _ _ _ _ _ _ _ _ _ _ _ _ _ _

_ _ _ _ _ _ _ _ _ _ _ _ _ _ _ _ _

_ _ _ _ _ _ _ _ _ _ _ _ _ _ _ _ _

_ _ _ _ _ _ _ _ _ _ _ _ _ _ _ _ _

My Quran Tracker

Surah: _ _ _ _ _ _ _ _ _ _ _ _ _ _

Verse: _ _ _ _ _ _ _ To: _ _ _ _ _ _

What I'm Grateful For Today

♥

♥

♥

♥

♥

Light up your "Salah" journey by adding a pop of color to each one you performed today

| Fajr | Duhr | Asr | Maghrib | Isha |

What I accomplished today: _

_ _

_ _

How I felt: _

_ _

_ _

Ramadan Acrostic Poem #4

An acrostic poem is a type of poem where the first letter of each line spells out a word or phrase. All lines should relate to or Describe the poem.

Write an acrostic poem for the word below

Iftar

I _____

F _____

T _____

A _____

R _____

Design Your Own Mosque

Unleash Your Creativity! you'll be the architect and designer, Build Your Own mosque Masterpiece!

Ramadan Day 28

My Fasting Today Was:

Part   Half   Most   Full

Good deeds I did today

_ _ _ _ _ _ _ _ _ _ _ _ _ _ _ _ _
_ _ _ _ _ _ _ _ _ _ _ _ _ _ _ _ _ _
_ _ _ _ _ _ _ _ _ _ _ _ _ _ _ _ _ _
_ _ _ _ _ _ _ _ _ _ _ _ _ _ _ _ _
_ _ _ _ _ _ _ _ _ _ _ _ _ _ _ _
_ _ _ _ _ _ _ _ _ _ _ _ _

My Quran Tracker

Surah: _ _ _ _ _ _ _ _ _ _ _ _ _ _ _ _

Verse: _ _ _ _ _ _ _ To: _ _ _ _ _ _

What I'm Grateful For Today

♥
♥
♥
♥
♥

Light up your "Salah" journey by adding a pop of color to each one you performed today

Fajr	Duhr	Asr	Maghrib	Isha

What I accomplished today: _ _ _ _ _ _ _ _ _ _ _
_ _
_ _

How I felt: _
_ _
_ _

Ramadan Math #3

Put your math skills to the test by solving these two-digit addition problems, using regrouping if needed

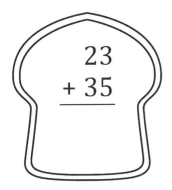
23
+ 35

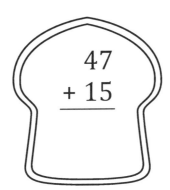
47
+ 15

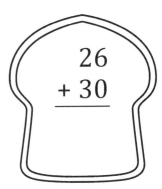
26
+ 30

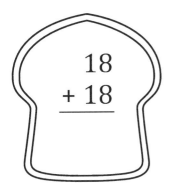
18
+ 18

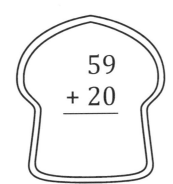
59
+ 20

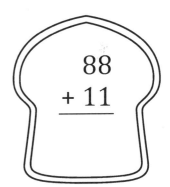
88
+ 11

37
+ 22

55
+ 44

17
+ 65

75
+ 15

12
+ 16

31
+ 32

Prophet Muhammad (pbuh)

Our prophet Muhammad (pbuh) was born in Mecca in 570 AD. His father had passed away before he was born and his mother passed away when he was just seven years old. After his mother's passing, his grandfather and then his uncle took care of him and raised him as their own.

As he grew up, Prophet Muhammad (pbuh) was known for his honesty and trustworthiness. He never participated in the wrong activities and was well respected in Mecca. A wealthy woman named Khadija heard of his reputation and asked him to trade for her. She was so impressed by his character that she asked him to marry her and he agreed.

When Prophet Muhammad (pbuh) was 40 years old, he went to the Hira mountain near Mecca to worship Allah (SWT) and think about His wonders. It was there that he received his first revelation from the Angel Jibril. Over time, the revelations continued to come, instructing him to spread the teachings of Islam and invite people to worship Allah (SWT) and leave behind idol worship.

Prophet Muhammad (pbuh) faced intense hostility from the idol worshipers in Mecca when he started openly spreading Islam, but there were also people who believed in him. Despite the punishment and abuse from the leaders of Mecca, Allah (SWT) protected him so he could continue spreading the message.

When his call was rejected in Mecca, he migrated to Medina where he was welcomed and founded the first mosque, the Quba mosque. The idol worshipers of Mecca eventually led their armies to attack Medina, but the Muslims were victorious. The idol worshipers signed a treaty to stop fighting, but it didn't last long and after a small group of horsemen from Mecca attacked the Muslims, the treaty was cancelled.

In just a few short years, most of the Arab Peninsula became Muslims and followed Prophet Muhammad (pbuh) to conquer Mecca. When they arrived, they broke the idols and forgave the people. Bilal climbed to the top of the Kaaba and called for prayer, marking a great victory for Prophet Muhammad (pbuh) in spreading Islam throughout the Arab Peninsula.

Prophet Muhammad (pbuh) passed away on June 8, 632, but his legacy lived on through his teachings and the leadership of his friend Abu Bakr who became the first caliph.

The story of Prophet Muhammad (pbuh) teaches us about his kindness, wisdom, bravery, and devotion to Allah.

Ramadan Day 29

My Fasting Today Was:

Part   Half   Most   Full

Good deeds I did today

_____
_____
_____
_____
_____
_____

My Quran Tracker

Surah: _____

Verse: _____ To: _____

What I'm Grateful For Today

♥ _____

♥ _____

♥ _____

♥ _____

♥ _____

Light up your "Salah" journey by adding a pop of color to each one you performed today

| Fajr | Duhr | Asr | Maghrib | Isha |

What I accomplished today: _____
_____
_____

How I felt: _____
_____
_____

Word Search #5

Get your eyes and brains ready, because it's time to search for hidden words related to Ramadan! Can you find them all?

```
B B Q O U F G E E U S
O I L Q X R Q T K A A
W S F W W A A R T R J
U M S A J H K D I K A
H I Y K P F Y J M A D
H L J I T R E J U S A
O L L K A H A M B K H
M A P S W C A B A T B
C H O B H M R L R T S
D R Z J I X T C A F W
T R D E D S M L K L Q
```

Hejira   Caliphate   Tawhid

Halal   Imam   Rosary

Bismillah   Mubarak   Sajadah

Ramadan Math #4

Brew up a storm of math mastery! Use the numbers on the teapot to fill in the circles, mix in some multiplication, and create the perfect equation.

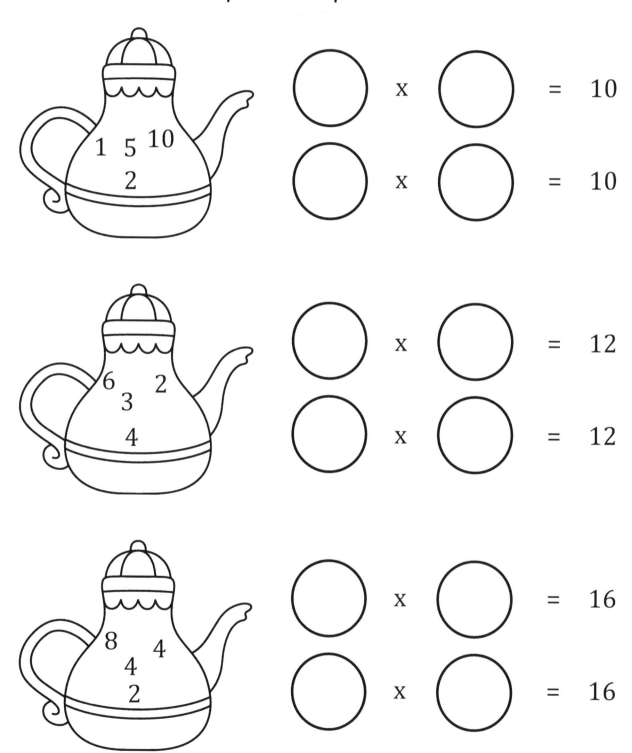

$\bigcirc$ x $\bigcirc$ = 10

$\bigcirc$ x $\bigcirc$ = 10

1 5 10
2

$\bigcirc$ x $\bigcirc$ = 12

$\bigcirc$ x $\bigcirc$ = 12

6 2
3
4

$\bigcirc$ x $\bigcirc$ = 16

$\bigcirc$ x $\bigcirc$ = 16

8 4
4
2

Ramadan Day 30

My Fasting Today Was:

Part Half Most Full

Good deeds I did today

_ _

_ _

_ _

_ _

_ _

_ _

_ _

My Quran Tracker

Surah: _ _ _ _ _ _ _ _ _ _ _ _ _ _ _

Verse: _ _ _ _ _ _ _ To: _ _ _ _ _ _ _

What I'm Grateful For Today

♥

♥

♥

♥

♥

Light up your "Salah" journey by adding a pop of color to each one you performed today

| Fajr | Duhr | Asr | Maghrib | Isha |

What I accomplished today: _

_ _

_ _

How I felt: _

_ _

_ _

Eid Greeting Card

Spread joy and happiness this Eid with your very own, handmade greeting card! Get creative and show your love to your family and friends

Reflecting on Ramadan

As the month of Ramadan comes to an end, it's a time to reflect on what we have learned and experienced over the past 30 days. By journaling our thoughts and feelings, we can remember the special moments and lessons we learned during this time.

Instructions:

Find a quiet place to sit and write.

Take a few deep breaths and think about your Ramadan experience.

Write down the answers to the following questions in your journal:

What did you learn about yourself during Ramadan?

What were some of your favorite parts of Ramadan?

How did you grow closer to Allah during this month?

What challenges did you face during Ramadan and how did you overcome them?

How will you continue to apply the lessons you learned during Ramadan in your daily life?

Tips:

Be honest with yourself and write what is truly in your heart.

Use colorful markers or stickers to make your journal entry special.

Share your journal with a family member or friend and talk about your Ramadan experience together.

By taking the time to reflect on our experiences during Ramadan, we can keep the lessons and blessings close to our hearts all year long.

Reflecting on Ramadan

Reflecting on Ramadan

Solutions

Word Search #1

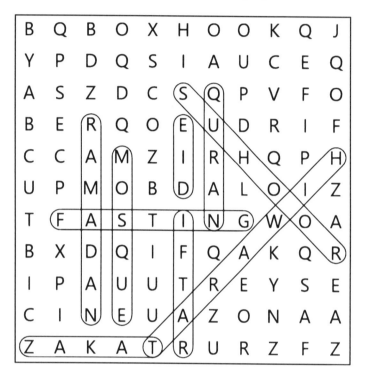

Ramadan Maze Craze

Ramadan Acrostic Poem #1
(possible answer)

Rays of hope shining bright

A special time of the year

Moments of prayer, love and light

Adoration and worship so dear

Days filled with patience and might

And nights of reflection and cheer

Islamic Nations Anagrams #1

Morocco = Coma or

Iran = Rain

Iraq = Qiara

Saudi Arabia = Carasia Dais

Tunisia = Sinatu

Libya = Labiy

Quran Quest

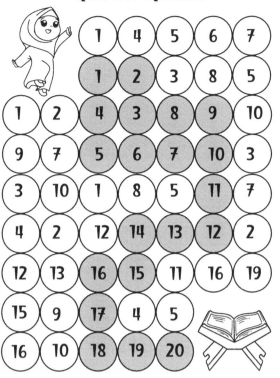

Ramadan Crossword #1

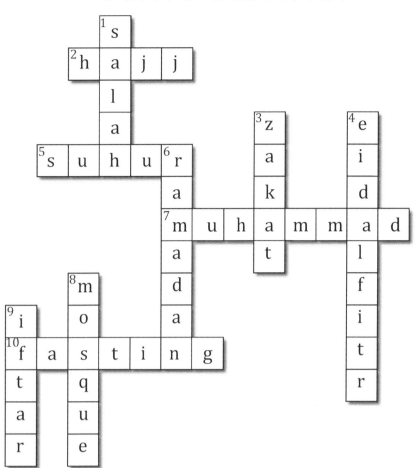

Word Search #2

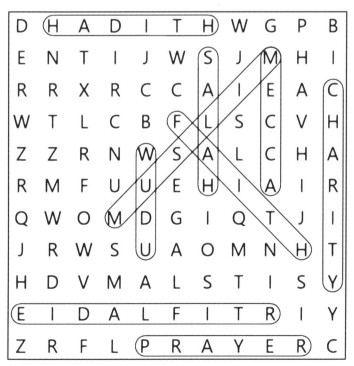

Hajj Maze

Ramadan Scramble Game #1

R a m a d a n

M u b a r a k

Ramadan Acrostic Poem #2
(possible answer)

Standing before the Lord so high

Actions of worship with all our might

Lifting our hearts to the sky

A prayer for peace, happiness, and light

Truly a journey to the divine

Islamic Nations Anagrams #2

Syria = Rayis

Egypt = Exgyt

Oman = Mano

United Arab Emirates = Aneleasti Ma Drubu

Yemen = Nemye

Bahrain = Ahabirn

Lantern Counting Activity

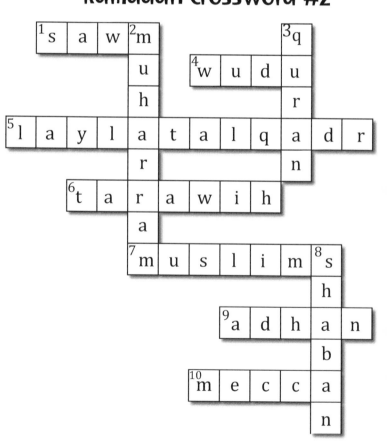

Ramadan Crossword #2

¹s	a	w	²m			³q			
			u		⁴w	u	d	u	
			h			r			
⁵l	a	y	l	a	t	a	l	q	a d r
			r			n			
⁶t	a	r	a	w	i	h			
			a						
⁷m	u	s	l	i	m	⁸s			
						h			
⁹a	d	h	a	n					
						b			
¹⁰m	e	c	c	a					
				n					

Word Search #3

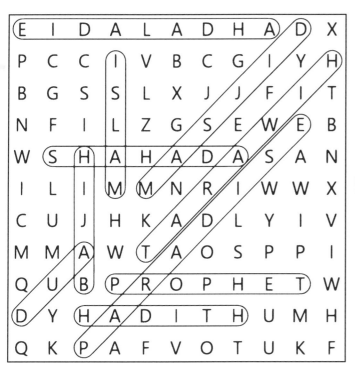

A Journey Through Ramadan

Islamic Months

Muḥarram

Ṣafar

Rabī ͑ al-Awwal

Rabī ͑ al-Thānī

Jumādā al-Awwal

Jumādā al-Thānī

Rajab

Sha ͑ bān

Ramaḍān

Shawwāl

Dhū al-Qa ͑ dah

Dhū al-Ḥijjah

Ramadan Scramble Game #2

Muslim Festivals

Ninth month in the Islamic calendar, devoted to fasting, prayer, and reflection	Ramadan
Marks the end of the month-long fasting period.	Eid al-Fitr
Commemorates the birth of Prophet Muhammad	Maulid Al-Nabi
Celebrated in memory of Prophet Ibrahim's willingness to sacrifice his son for Allah	Eid al-Adha
The night that the first verses of the Quran were revealed to Prophet Muhammad.	Lyalat al-Qadr

Ramadan Acrostic Poem #3
(possible answer)

Saying goodbye to food and drink

A time for reflection and self-think

Walking on the path of truth

Making a promise to stay in faith

More love and devotion in each breath

Word Search #4

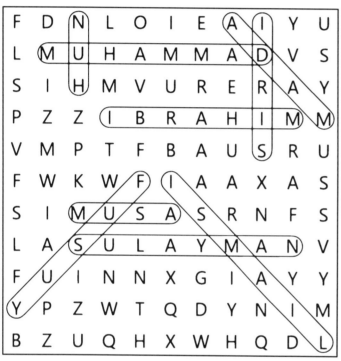

F	D	N	L	O	I	E	A	I	Y	U
L	M	U	H	A	M	M	A	D	V	S
S	I	H	M	V	U	R	E	R	A	Y
P	Z	Z	I	B	R	A	H	I	M	M
V	M	P	T	F	B	A	U	S	R	U
F	W	K	W	F	I	A	A	X	A	S
S	I	M	U	S	A	S	R	N	F	S
L	A	S	U	L	A	Y	M	A	N	V
F	U	I	N	N	X	G	I	A	Y	Y
Y	P	Z	W	T	Q	D	Y	N	I	M
B	Z	U	Q	H	X	W	H	Q	D	L

Ramadan Math #1

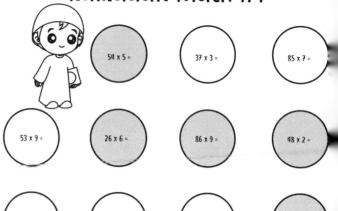

54 x 5 =

37 x 3 =

85 x 7 =

53 x 9 =

26 x 6 =

86 x 9 =

48 x 2 =

27 x 7 =

87 x 3 =

79 x 5 =

37 x 8 =

88 x 7 =

75 x 6 =

64 x 4 =

98 x 3 =

96 x 5 =

47 x 9 =

Ramadan Crossword #3

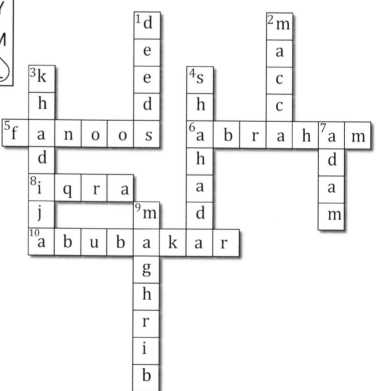

Noor's Sajadah Search

Ramadan Math #2

⊘ = 2

☾ = 4

▭ = 1

🕌 = 3

Islamic Nations Anagrams #3

Algeria = Agrlei

Lebanon = Bneonla

Sudan = Sandu

Jordan = Donjar

Kuwait = Twuak

Qatar = Tqara

Ramadan Acrostic Poem #4
(possible answer)

In the evening, the fast we break

Feasting on dates and food so sweet

Tasting the blessings we seek

And thanks to Allah, our hearts beat

Rejoicing in the company we meet

Ramadan Math #3

```
  23        47        26
+ 35      + 15      + 30
----      ----      ----
  58        62        56
```

```
  18        59        88
+ 18      + 20      + 11
----      ----      ----
  36        79        99
```

```
  37        55        17
+ 22      + 44      + 65
----      ----      ----
  59        99        82
```

```
  75        12        31
+ 15      + 16      + 32
----      ----      ----
  90        28        63
```

Word Search #5

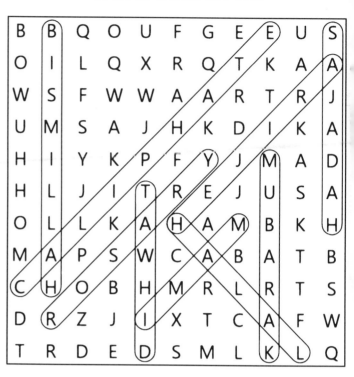

```
B  B  Q  O  U  F  G  E  E  U  S
O  I  L  Q  X  R  Q  T  K  A  A
W  S  F  W  W  A  A  R  T  R  J
U  M  S  A  J  H  K  D  I  K  A
H  I  Y  K  P  F  Y  J  M  A  D
H  L  J  I  T  R  E  J  U  S  A
O  L  L  K  A  H  A  M  B  K  H
M  A  P  S  W  C  A  B  A  T  B
C  H  O  B  H  M  R  L  R  T  S
D  R  Z  J  I  X  T  C  A  F  W
T  R  D  E  D  S  M  L  K  L  Q
```

Ramadan Math #4

10   x   1   =   10

5   x   2   =   10

6   x   2   =   12

3   x   4   =   12

8   x   2   =   16

4   x   4   =   16

Thank you for purchasing my activity book for kids!

I hope your child had fun completing the activities and that the book brought a little bit of fun and creativity into their day.

If you have a moment, I would really appreciate it if you could leave a review on Amazon. Your feedback helps other parents decide if the book is right for their children, and it helps me improve as a writer. Plus, it's always nice to hear what people think of my work!

Thank you in advance for your help, and I hope you and your child have a great day!

Kindest regards,

Jabir Al-Zahir

Made in United States
Troutdale, OR
03/11/2024

18377528R00060